D1602886

Poems of Passion

Ella Wheeler Wilcox

IndoEuropean
Publishing.com
Los Angeles, CA, USA

Oh, you who read some song that I have sung,
What know you of the soul from whence it sprung?

Dost dream the poet ever speaks aloud
His secret thought unto the listening crowd?

Go take the murmuring sea-shell from the shore:
You have its shape, its color and no more.

It tells not one of those vast mysteries
That lie beneath the surface of the seas.

Our songs are shells, cast out by-waves of thought;
Here, take them at your pleasure; but think not

You've seen beneath the surface of the waves,
Where lie our shipwrecks and our coral caves.

PREFACE

Among the twelve hundred poems which have emanated from my too prolific pen there are some forty or fifty which treat entirely of that emotion which has been denominated "the grand passion"—love. A few of those are of an extremely fiery character.

When I issued my collection known as "Maurine, and Other Poems," I purposely omitted all save two or three of these. I had been frequently accused of writing only sentimental verses; and I took pleasure and pride in presenting to the public a volume which contained more than one hundred poems upon other than sentimental topics. But no sooner was the book published than letters of regret came to me from friends and strangers, and from all quarters of the globe, asking why this or that love poem had been omitted. These regrets were repeated to me by so many people that I decided to collect and issue these poems in a small volume to be called "Poems of Passion." By the word "Passion" I meant the "grand passion" of love. To those who take exception to the title of the book I would suggest an early reference to Webster's definitions of the word.

Since this volume has caused so much agitation throughout the entire country, and even sent a tremor across the Atlantic into the Old World, I beg leave to make a few statements concerning some of the poems.

The excitement of mingled horror and amaze seems to center upon four poems, namely: "Delilah," "Ad Finem," "Conversion," and "Communism."

"Delilah" was written and first published in 1877. I had been reading history, and became stirred by the power of such women as Aspasia and Cleopatra over such grand men as Antony, Socrates, and Pericles. Under the influence of this feeling I dashed off "Delilah," which I meant to be an expression of the powerful fascination of such a woman upon the memory of a man, even as he neared the hour of death. If the poem is immoral, then the history which inspired it is immoral. I consider it my finest effort.

"Ad Finem" was written in 1878. I think there are few women of strong character and affections who cannot, from either experience or observation, understand the violent intensity of regret and despair which sometimes takes possession of the human heart after the loss by death, fate, or the force of circumstances, of some one very dear.

In "Ad Finem" I intended to give voice to this very common experience of almost every heart. Many noble women have since told me that the poem was true to life. It is not, as many people have wilfully or stupidly construed it, a bit of poetical advice to womankind to "barter the joys of Paradise" for "just one kiss." It is simply an illustration of a moment of turbulent anguish and vehement despair, such moments of unreasoning and overwhelming sorrow as the most moral people may experience during a lifetime.

In "Communism" I endeavored to use a new simile in illustrating that somewhat hackneyed theme of the supremacy of Love over Reason; and simply to carry out my idea I represented the violent uprising of the Communist emotions against King Reason.

"Conversion" was suggested to me by the remark of a gentleman friend. In speaking to me of the woman he loved, he said: "I have always been a skeptic regarding the existence of heaven, but I am so much happier in my love for this woman than I ever supposed it possible for me to be on earth that I begin to believe that the tales of heavenly raptures may be true."

I embodied his idea in the poem which has brought, with a few others, so much censure and criticism upon this volume, although it contains nearly seventy-five other selections quite irreproachable in character, however faulty they may be in construction.

It is impossible to pursue a successful literary career and follow the advice of all one's "best friends." I have received severe censure from my orthodox friends for writing liberal verses. My liberal friends condemn my devout and religious poems as "aiding superstition." My early temperance verses were pronounced "fanatical trash" by others.

With all due thanks and appreciation for the kind motives which interest so many dear friends in my career, I yet feel compelled to follow the light which my own intellect and judgment cast upon my way, rather than any one of the many conflicting rays which other minds would lend me.

ELLA WHEELER

CONTENTS

MISCELLANEOUS POEMS

LOVE'S LANGUAGE

How does Love speak?
In the faint flush upon the tell-tale cheek,
And in the pallor that succeeds it; by
The quivering lid of an averted eye—
The smile that proves the patent to a sigh—
Thus doth Love speak.

How does Love speak?
By the uneven heart-throbs, and the freak
Of bounding pulses that stand still and ache,
While new emotions, like strange barges, make
Along vein-channels their disturbing course;
Still as the dawn, and with the dawn's swift force—
Thus doth Love speak.

How does Love speak?
In the avoidance of that which we seek—
The sudden silence and reserve when near—
The eye that glistens with an unshed tear—
The joy that seems the counterpart of fear,
As the alarmed heart leaps in the breast,
And knows and names and greets its godlike guest—
Thus doth Love speak.

How does Love speak?
In the proud spirit suddenly grown meek—
The haughty heart grown humble; in the tender
And unnamed light that floods the world with splendor;
In the resemblance which the fond eyes trace
In all fair things to one beloved face;
In the shy touch of hands that thrill and tremble;
In looks and lips that can no more dissemble—
Thus doth Love speak.

How does Love speak?
In the wild words that uttered seem so weak
They shrink ashamed to silence; in the fire
Glance strikes with glance, swift flashing high and higher
Like lightnings that precede the mighty storm;
In the deep, soulful stillness; in the warm,
Impassioned tide that sweeps through throbbing veins
Between the shores of keen delight and pains;
In the embrace where madness melts in bliss,
And in the convulsive rapture of a kiss—
Thus doth Love speak.

IMPATIENCE

How can I wait until you come to me?
The once fleet mornings linger by the way,
Their sunny smiles touched with malicious glee
At my unrest; they seem to pause, and play
Like truant children, while I sigh and say,
How can I wait?

How can I wait? Of old, the rapid hours
Refused to pause or loiter with me long;
But now they idly fill their hands with flowers,
And make no haste, but slowly stroll among
The summer blooms, not heeding my one song,
How can I wait?

How can I wait? The nights alone are kind;
They reach forth to a future day, and bring
Sweet dreams of you to people all my mind;
And time speeds by on light and airy wing.
I feast upon your face, I no more sing,
How can I wait?

How can I wait? The morning breaks the spell
A pitying night has flung upon my soul.
You are not near me, and I know full well
My heart has need of patience and control;
Before we meet, hours, days, and weeks must roll.
How can I wait?

How can I wait? Oh, love, how can I wait
Until the sunlight of your eyes shall shine
Upon my world that seems so desolate?
Until your hand-clasp warms my blood like wine;
Until you come again, oh, love of mine,
How can I wait?

COMMUNISM

When my blood flows calm as a purling river,
When my heart is asleep and my brain has sway,
It is then that I vow we must part forever,
That I will forget you, and put you away
Out of my life, as a dream is banished
Out of the mind when the dreamer awakes;
That I know it will be, when the spell has vanished,
Better for both of our sakes.

When the court of the mind is ruled by Reason,
I know it is wiser for us to part;
But Love is a spy who is plotting treason,
In league with that warm, red rebel, the Heart.
They whisper to me that the King is cruel,
That his reign is wicked, his law a sin;
And every word they utter is fuel
To the flame that smoulders within.

And on nights like this, when my blood runs riot
With the fever of youth and its mad desires,
When my brain in vain bids my heart be quiet,
When my breast seems the centre of lava-fires,
Oh, then is the time when most I miss you,
And I swear by the stars and my soul and say
That I will have you and hold you and kiss you,
Though the whole world stands in the way.

And like Communists, as mad, as disloyal,
My fierce emotions roam out of their lair;
They hate King Reason for being royal;
They would fire his castle, and burn him there.
Oh, Love! they would clasp you and crush you and kill you,
In the insurrection of uncontrol.

Across the miles, does this wild war thrill you
That is raging in my soul?

THE COMMON LOT

It is a common fate—a woman's lot—
To waste on one the riches of her soul,
Who takes the wealth she gives him, but cannot
Repay the interest, and much less the whole.

As I look up into your eyes and wait
For some response to my fond gaze and touch,
It seems to me there is no sadder fate
Than to be doomed to loving overmuch.

Are you not kind? Ah, yes, so very kind—
So thoughtful of my comfort, and so true.
Yes, yes, dear heart; but I, not being blind,
Know that I am not loved as I love you.

One tenderer word, a little longer kiss,
Will fill my soul with music and with song;
And if you seem abstracted, or I miss
The heart-tone from your voice, my world goes wrong.

And oftentimes you think me childish—weak—
When at some thoughtless word the tears will start;
You cannot understand how aught you speak
Has power to stir the depths of my poor heart.

I cannot help it, dear,—I wish I could,
Or feign indifference where I now adore;
For if I seemed to love you less you would,
Manlike, I have no doubt, love me the more.

'Tis a sad gift, that much applauded thing,
A constant heart; for fact doth daily prove
That constancy finds oft a cruel sting,
While fickle natures win the deeper love.

INDIVIDUALITY

O yes, I love you, and with all my heart;
Just as a weaker woman loves her own,
Better than I love my beloved art,
Which, till you came, reigned royally, alone,
My king, my master. Since I saw your face
I have dethroned it, and you hold that place.

I am as weak as other women are:
Your frown can make the whole world like a tomb;
Your smile shines brighter than the sun, by far.
Sometimes I think there is not space or room
In all the earth for such a love as mine,
And it soars up to breathe in realms divine.

I know that your desertion or neglect
Could break my heart, as women's hearts do break.
If my wan days had nothing to expect
From your love's splendor, all joy would forsake
The chambers of my soul. Yes, this is true.
And yet, and yet—one thing I keep from you.

There is a subtle part of me, which went
Into my long pursued and worshipped art;
Though your great love fills me with such content
No other love finds room now, in my heart.
Yet that rare essence was my art's alone.
Thank God, you cannot grasp it; 'tis mine own.

Thank God, I say, for while I love you so,
With that vast love, as passionate as tender,
I feel an exultation as I know
I have not made you a complete surrender.
Here is my body; bruise it, if you will,
And break my heart; I have that *something* still.

You cannot grasp it. Seize the breath of morn
Or bind the perfume of the rose, as well.
God put it in my soul when I was born;
It is not mine to give away, or sell,
Or offer up on any altar shrine.
It was my art's; and when not art's, 'tis mine,

For love's sake I can put the art away,
Or anything which stands 'twixt me and you.
But that strange essence God bestowed, I say,
To permeate the work He gave to do:
And it cannot be drained, dissolved, or sent
Through any channel save the one He meant.

FRIENDSHIP AFTER LOVE

After the fierce midsummer all ablaze
Has burned itself to ashes, and expires
In the intensity of its own fires,
There come the mellow, mild, St. Martin days,
Crowned with the calm of peace, but sad with haze.
So after Love has led us, till he tires
Of his own throes and torments and desires,
Comes large-eyed friendship: with a restful gaze
He beckons us to follow, and across
Cool, verdant vales we wander free from care.
Is it a touch of frost lies in the air?
Why are we haunted with a sense of loss?
We do not wish the pain back, or the heat;
And yet, and yet, these days are incomplete.

QUERIES

Well, how has it been with you since we met
That last strange time of a hundred times?
When we met to swear that we could forget—
I your caresses, and you my rhymes—
The rhyme of my lays that rang like a bell,
And the rhyme of my heart with yours, as well?

How has it been since we drank that last kiss,
That was bitter with lees of the wasted wine,
When the tattered remains of a threadbare bliss,
And the worn-out shreds of a joy divine,
With a year's best dreams and hopes, were cast
Into the rag-bag of the Past?

Since Time, the rag-buyer, hurried away,
With a chuckle of glee at a bargain made,
Did you discover, like me, one day,
That, hid in the folds of those garments frayed,
Were priceless jewels and diadems—
The soul's best treasures, the heart's best gems?

Have you, too, found that you could not supply
The place of those jewels so rare and chaste?
Do all that you borrow or beg or buy
Prove to be nothing but skilful paste?
Have you found pleasure, as I found art,
Not all-sufficient to fill your heart?

Do you sometimes sigh for the tattered shreds
Of the old delight that we cast away,
And find no worth in the silken threads
Of newer fabrics we wear to-day?
Have you thought the bitter of that last kiss
Better than sweets of a later bliss?

What idle queries!—or yes or no—
Whatever your answer, I understand
That there is no pathway by which we can go
Back to the dead past's wonderland;
And the gems he purchased from me, from you,
There is no rebuying from Time, the Jew.

UPON THE SAND

All love that has not friendship for its base
Is like a mansion built upon the sand.
Though brave its walls as any in the land,
And its tall turrets lift their heads in grace;
Though skilful and accomplished artists trace
Most beautiful designs on every hand,
And gleaming statues in dim niches stand,
And fountains play in some flow'r-hidden place:

Yet, when from the frowning east a sudden gust
Of adverse fate is blown, or sad rains fall,
Day in, day out, against its yielding wall,
Lo! the fair structure crumbles to the dust.
Love, to endure life's sorrow and earth's woe,
Needs friendship's solid mason-work below.

REUNITED

Let us begin, dear love, where we left off;
Tie up the broken threads of that old dream,
And go on happy as before, and seem
Lovers again, though all the world may scoff.

Let us forget the graves which lie between
Our parting and our meeting, and the tears
That rusted out the gold-work of the years,
The frosts that fell upon our gardens green.

Let us forget the cold, malicious Fate
Who made our loving hearts her idle toys,
And once more revel in the old sweet joys
Of happy love. Nay, it is not too late!

Forget the deep-ploughed furrows in my brow;
Forget the silver gleaming in my hair;
Look only in my eyes! Oh! darling, there
The old love shone no warmer then than now.

Down in the tender deeps of thy dear eyes
I find the lost sweet memory of my youth,
Bright with the holy radiance of thy truth,
And hallowed with the blue of summer skies.

Tie up the broken threads and let us go,
Like reunited lovers, hand in hand,
Back, and yet onward, to the sunny land
Of our To Be, which was our Long Ago.

WHAT SHALL WE DO?

Here now forevermore our lives must part.
My path leads there, and yours another way.
What shall we do with this fond love, dear heart?
It grows a heavier burden day by day.

Hide it? In all earth's caverns, void and vast,
There is not room enough to hide it, dear;
Not even the mighty storehouse of the past
Could cover it from our own eyes, I fear.

Drown it? Why, were the contents of each ocean
Merged into one great sea, too shallow then
Would be its waters to sink this emotion
So deep it could not rise to life again.

Burn it? In all the furnace flames below,
It would not in a thousand years expire.
Nay! it would thrive, exult, expand, and grow,
For from its very birth it fed on fire.

Starve it? Yes, yes, that is the only way.
Give it no food, of glance, or word, or sigh;
No memories, even, of any bygone day;
No crumbs of vain regrets—so let it die.

"THE BEAUTIFUL BLUE DANUBE"

They drift down the hall together;
He smiles in her lifted eyes;
Like waves of that mighty river,
The strains of the "Danube" rise.
They float on its rhythmic measure
Like leaves on a summer-stream;
And here, in this scene of pleasure,
I bury my sweet, dead dream.

Through the cloud of her dusky tresses,
Like a star, shines out her face,
And the form his strong arm presses
Is sylph like in its grace.
As a leaf on the bounding river
Is lost in the seething sea,
I know that forever and ever
My dream is lost to me.

And still the viols are playing
That grand old wordless rhyme;
And still those two ate swaying
In perfect tune and time.
If the great bassoons that mutter,
If the clarinets that blow,
Were given a voice to utter
The secret things they know,

Would the lists of the slam who slumber
On the Danube's battle-plains
The unknown hosts outnumber
Who die 'neath the "Danube's" strains?
Those fall where cannons rattle,
'Mid the rain of shot and shell;

But these, in a fiercer battle,
Find death in the music's swell.

With the river's roar of passion
Is blended the dying groan;
But here, in the halls of fashion,
Hearts break, and make no moan.
And the music, swelling and sweeping,
Like the river, knows it all;
But none are counting or keeping
The lists of these who fall.

ANSWERED

Good-bye—yes, I am going.
Sudden? Well, you are right;
But a startling truth came home to me
With sudden force last night.
What is it? Shall I tell you?
Nay, that is why I go.
I am running away from the battlefield
Turning my back on the foe.

Riddles? You think me cruel!
Have you not been most kind?
Why, when you question me like that,
What answer can I find?
You fear you failed to amuse me,
Your husband's friend and guest,
Whom he bade you entertain and please—
Well, you have done your best.
Then why am I going?
A friend of mine abroad,
Whose theories I have been acting upon,
Has proven himself a fraud.
You have heard me quote from Plato
A thousand times no doubt;
Well, I have discovered he did not know
What he was talking about.

You think I am speaking strangely?
You cannot understand?
Well, let me look down into your eyes,
And let me take your hand.
I am running away from danger;
I am flying before I fall;
I am going because with heart and soul

I love you—that is all.
There, now you are white with anger;
I knew it would be so.
You should not question a man too close
When he tells you he must go.

THROUGH THE VALLEY

[AFTER JAMES THOMSON]

As I came through the Valley of Despair,
As I came through the valley, on my sight,
More awful than the darkness of the night,
Shone glimpses of a Past that had been fair,
And memories of eyes that used to smile,
And wafts of perfume from a vanished isle,
As I came through the valley.

As I came through the valley I could see,
As I came through the valley, fair and far,
As drowning men look up and see a star,
The fading shore of my lost Used-to-be;
And like an arrow in my heart I heard
The last sad notes of Hope's expiring bird,
As I came through the valley.

As I came through the valley desolate,
As I came through the valley, like a beam
Of lurid lightning I beheld a gleam
Of Love's great eyes that now were full of hate.
Dear God! Dear God! I could bear all but that;
But I fell down soul-stricken, dead, thereat,
As I came through the valley.

BUT ONE

The year has but one June, dear friend;
The year has but one June;
And when that perfect month doth end,
The robin's song, though loud, though long,
Seems never quite in tune.

The rose, though still its blushing face
By bee and bird is seen,
May yet have lost that subtle grace—
That nameless spell the winds know
Which makes it garden's queen.

Life's perfect June, love's red, red rose,
Have burned and bloomed for me.
Though still youth's summer sunlight glows;
Though thou art kind, dear friend, I find
I have no heart for thee.

GUILO

Yes, yes! I love thee, Guilo; thee alone.
Why dost thou sigh, and wear that face of sorrow?
The sunshine is to-day's, although it shone
On yesterday, and may shine on to-morrow.

I love but thee, my Guilo! be content;
The greediest heart can claim but present pleasure.
The future is thy God's. The past is spent.
To-day is thine; clasp close the precious treasure.

See how I love thee, Guilo! Lips and eyes
Could never under thy fond gaze dissemble.
I could not feign these passion-laden sighs;
Deceiving thee, my pulses would not tremble.

"So I loved Romney." Hush, thou foolish one—
I should forget him wholly wouldst thou let me;
Or but remember that his day was done
From that supremest hour when first I met thee.

"And Paul?" Well, what of Paul? Paul had blue eyes,
And Romney gray, and thine are darkly tender!
One finds fresh feelings under change of skies—
A new horizon brings a newer splendor.

As I love thee I never loved before;
Believe me, Guilo, for I speak most truly.
What though to Romney and to Paul I swore
The self-same words; my heart now worships newly.

We never feel the same emotion twice:
No two ships ever ploughed the self-same billow;
The waters change with every fall and rise;
So, Guilo, go contented to thy pillow.

THE DUET

I was smoking a cigarette;
Maud, my wife, and the tenor, McKey,
Were singing together a blithe duet,
And days it were better I should forget
Came suddenly back to me—
Days when life seemed a gay masque ball,
And to love and be loved was the sum of it all.

As they sang together, the whole scene fled,
The room's rich hangings, the sweet home air,
Stately Maud, with her proud blond head,
And I seemed to see in her place instead
A wealth of blue-black hair,
And a face, ah! your face—yours, Lisette;
A face it were wiser I should forget.

We were back—well, no matter when or where;
But you remember, I know, Lisette.
I saw you, dainty and debonair,
With the very same look that you used to wear
In the days I should forget.
And your lips, as red as the vintage we quaffed,
Were pearl-edged bumpers of wine when you laughed.

Two small slippers with big rosettes
Peeped out under your kilt skirt there,
While we sat smoking our cigarettes
(Oh, I shall be dust when my heart forgets')
And singing that self-same an,
And between the verses, for interlude,
I kissed your throat and your shoulders nude.

You were so full of a subtle file,
You were so warm and so sweet, Lisette;

You were everything men admire,
And there were no fetters to make us tire,
For you were—a pretty grisette.
But you loved, as only such natures can,
With a love that makes heaven or hell for a man.

They have ceased singing that old duet,
Stately Maud and the tenor, McKey.
"You are burning your coat with your cigarette,
And *qu' avez vous*, dearest, your lids are wet,"
Maud says, as she leans o'er me.
And I smile, and lie to her, husband-wise,
"Oh, it is nothing but smoke in my eyes."

LITTLE QUEEN

Do you remember the name I wore—
The old pet-name of Little Queen—
In the dear, dead days that are no more,
The happiest days of our lives, I ween?
For we loved with that passionate love of youth
That blesses but once with its perfect bliss—
A love that, in spite of its trust and truth,
Seems never to thrive in a world like this.

I lived for you, and you lived for me;
All was centered in "Little Queen;"
And never a thought in our hearts had we
That strife or trouble could come between.
What utter sinking of self it was!
How little we cared for the world of men!
For love's fair kingdom and love's sweet laws
Were all of the world and life to us then.

But a love like ours was a challenge to Fate;
She rang down the curtain and shifted the scene;
Yet sometimes now, when the day grows late,
I can hear you calling for Little Queen;
For a happy home and a busy life
Can never wholly crowd out our past;
In the twilight pauses that come from strife,
You will think of me while life shall last.

And however sweet the voice of fame
May sing to me of a great world's praise,
I shall long sometimes for the old pet-name
That you gave to me in the dear, dead days;
And nothing the angel band can say,
When I reach the shores of the great Unseen,

Can please me so much as on that day
To hear your greeting of "Little Queen.

WHEREFORE?

Wherefore in dreams are sorrows borne anew,
A healed wound opened, or the past revived?
Last night in my deep sleep I dreamed of you;
Again the old love woke in me, and thrived
On looks of fire, and kisses, and sweet words
Like silver waters purling in a stream,
Or like the amorous melodies of birds:
A dream—a dream!

Again upon the glory of the scene
There settled that dread shadow of the cross
That, when hearts love too well, falls in between;
That warns them of impending woe and loss.
Again I saw you drifting from my life,
As barques are rudely parted in a stream;
Again my heart was torn with awful strife:
A dream—a dream!

Again the deep night settled on me there,
Alone I groped, and heard strange waters roll,
Lost in that blackness of supreme despair
That comes but once to any living soul.
Alone, afraid, I called your name aloud—
Mine eyes, unveiled, beheld white stars agleam,
And lo! awake, I cried, "Thank God, thank God!
A dream—a dream!"

DELILAH

In the midnight of darkness and terror,
When I would grope nearer to God,
With my back to a record of error
And the highway of sin I have trod,
There come to me shapes I would banish—
The shapes of the deeds I have done;
And I pray and I plead till they vanish—
All vanish and leave me, save one.

That one with a smile like the splendor
Of the sun in the middle-day skies—
That one with a spell that is tender—
That one with a dream in her eyes—
Cometh close, in her rare Southern beauty,
Her languor, her indolent grace;
And my soul turns its back on its duty,
To live in the light of her face.

She touches my cheek, and I quiver—
I tremble with exquisite pains;
She sighs—like an overcharged river
My blood rushes on through my veins',
She smiles—and in mad-tiger fashion,
As a she-tiger fondles her own,
I clasp her with fierceness and passion,
And kiss her with shudder and groan.

Once more, in our love's sweet beginning,
I put away God and the World;
Once more, in the joys of our sinning,
Are the hopes of eternity hurled.
There is nothing my soul lacks or misses
As I clasp the dream shape to my breast;

In the passion and pain of her kisses
Life blooms to its richest and best.

O ghost of dead sin unrelenting,
Go back to the dust and the sod!
Too dear and too sweet for repenting,
Ye stand between me and my God.
If I, by the Throne, should behold you,
Smiling up with those eyes loved so well,
Close, close in my arms I would fold you,
And drop with you down to sweet Hell!

LOVE SONG

Once in the world's first prime,
When nothing lived or stirred—
Nothing but new-born Time,
Nor was there even a bird—
The Silence spoke to a Star;
But I do not dare repeat
What it said to its love afar,
It was too sweet, too sweet.

But there, in the fair world's youth,
Ere sorrow had drawn breath,
When nothing was known but Truth,
Nor was there even death,
The Star to Silence was wed,
And the Sun was priest that day,
And they made their bridal-bed
High in the Milky Way.

For the great white star had heard
Her silent lover's speech;
It needed no passionate word
To pledge them each to each.
Oh, lady fair and far,
Hear, oh, hear and apply!
Thou, the beautiful Star—
The voiceless Silence, I.

TIME AND LOVE

Time flies. The swift hours hurry by
And speed us on to untried ways;
New seasons ripen, perish, die,
And yet love stays.
The old, old love—like sweet, at first,
At last like bitter wine—
I know not if it blest or curst
Thy life and mine.

Time flies. In vain our prayers, our tears!
We cannot tempt him to delays;
Down to the past he bears the years,
And yet love stays.
Through changing task and varying dream
We hear the same refrain,
As one can hear a plaintive theme
Run through each strain.

Time flies. He steals our pulsing youth;
He robs us of our care-free days;
He takes away our trust and truth:
And yet love stays.
O Time! take love! When love is vain,
When all its best joys die—
When only its regrets remain—
Let love, too, fly.

CHANGE

Changed? Yes, I will confess it—I have changed.
I do not love in the old fond way.
I am your friend still—time has not estranged
One kindly feeling of that vanished day.

But the bright glamour which made life a dream,
The rapture of that time, its sweet content,
Like visions of a sleeper's brain they seem—
And yet I cannot tell you how they went.

Why do you gaze with such accusing eyes
Upon me, dear? Is it so very strange
That hearts, like all things underneath God's skies
Should sometimes feel the influence of change?

The birds, the flowers, the foliage of the trees,
The stars which seem so fixed and so sublime,
Vast continents and the eternal seas—
All these do change with ever-changing time.

The face our mirror shows us year on year
Is not the same; our dearest aim or need,
Our lightest thought or feeling, hope or fear,
All, all the law of alteration heed.

How can we ask the human heart to stay
Content with fancies of Youth's earliest hours?
The year outgrows the violets of May,
Although, maybe, there are no fairer flowers.

And life may hold no sweeter love than this,
Which lies so cold, so voiceless, and so dumb.
And shall I miss it, dear? Why, yes, we miss
The violets always—till the roses come!

DESOLATION

I think that the bitterest sorrow or pain
Of love unrequited, or cold death's woe,
Is sweet compared to that hour when we know
That some grand passion is on the wane;

When we see that the glory and glow and grace
Which lent a splendor to night and day
Are surely fading, and showing the gray
And dull groundwork of the commonplace;

When fond expressions on dull ears fall,
When the hands clasp calmly without one thrill,
When we cannot muster by force of will
The old emotions that came at call;

When the dream has vanished we fain would keep,
When the heart, like a watch, runs out of gear,
And all the savor goes out of the year,
Oh, then is the time—if we can—to weep!

But no tears soften this dull, pale woe;
We must sit and face it with dry, sad eyes.
If we seek to hold it, the swifter joy flies—
We can only be passive, and let it go.

ISAURA

Dost thou not tire, Isaura, of this play?
"What play?" Why, this old play of winning hearts!
Nay, now, lift not thine eyes in that feigned way:
'Tis all in vain—I know thee and thine arts.

Let us be frank, Isaura. I have made
A study of thee; and while I admire
The practised skill with which thy plans are laid,
I can but wonder if thou dost not tire.

Why, I tire even of Hamlet and Macbeth!
When overlong the season runs, I find
Those master-scenes of passion, blood, and death,
After a time do pall upon my mind.

Dost thou not tire of lifting up thine eyes
To read the story thou hast read so oft—
Of ardent glances and deep quivering sighs,
Of haughty faces suddenly grown soft?

Is it not stale, oh, very stale, to thee,
The scene that follows? Hearts are much the same;
The loves of men but vary in degree—
They find no new expressions for the flame.

Thou must know all they utter ere they speak,
As I know Hamlet's part, whoever plays.
Oh, does it not seem sometimes poor and weak?
I think thou must grow weary of their ways.

I pity thee, Isaura! I would be
The humblest maiden with her dream untold
Rather than live a Queen of Hearts, like thee,
And find life's rarest treasures stale and old.

I pity thee; for now, let come what may,
Fame, glory, riches, yet life will lack all.
Wherewith can salt be salted? And what way
Can life be seasoned after love doth pall?

THE COQUETTE

Alone she sat with her accusing heart,
That, like a restless comrade frightened sleep,
And every thought that found her, left a dart
That hurt her so, she could not even weep.

Her heart that once had been a cup well filled
With love's red wine, save for some drops of gall
She knew was empty; though it had not spilled
Its sweets for one, but wasted them on all.

She stood upon the grave of her dead truth,
And saw her soul's bright armor red with rust,
And knew that all the riches of her youth
Were Dead Sea apples, crumbling into dust.

Love that had turned to bitter, biting scorn,
Hearthstones despoiled, and homes made desolate,
Made her cry out that she was ever born,
To loathe her beauty and to curse her fate.

NEW AND OLD

I and new love, in all its living bloom,
Sat vis-a-vis, while tender twilight hours
Went softly by us, treading as on flowers.
Then suddenly I saw within the room
The old love, long since lying in its tomb.
It dropped the cerecloth from its fleshless face
And smiled on me, with a remembered grace
That, like the noontide, lit the gloaming's gloom.

Upon its shroud there hung the grave's green mould,
About it hung the odor of the dead;
Yet from its cavernous eyes such light was shed
That all my life seemed gilded, as with gold;
Unto the trembling new love "'Go," I said
"I do not need thee, for I have the old."

NOT QUITE THE SAME

Not quite the same the spring-time seems to me,
Since that sad season when in separate ways
Our paths diverged. There are no more such days
As dawned for us in that lost time when we
Dwelt in the realm of dreams, illusive dreams;
Spring may be just as fair now, but it seems
Not quite the same.

Not quite the same is life, since we two parted,
Knowing it best to go our ways alone.
Fair measures of success we both have known,
And pleasant hours, and yet something departed
Which gold, nor fame, nor anything we win
Can all replace. And either life has been
Not quite the same.

Love is not quite the same, although each heart
Has formed new ties that are both sweet and true,
But that wild rapture, which of old we knew,
Seems to have been a something set apart
With that lost dream. There is no passion, now,
Mixed with this later love, which seems, somehow,
Not quite the same.

Not quite the same am I. My inner being
Reasons and knows that all is for the best.
Yet vague regrets stir always in my breast,
As my soul's eyes turn sadly backward, seeing
The vanished self that evermore must be,
This side of what we call eternity,
Not quite the same.

FROM THE GRAVE

When the first sere leaves of the year were falling,
I heard, with a heart that was strangely thrilled,
Out of the grave of a dead Past calling,
A voice I fancied forever stilled.

All through winter and spring and summer,
Silence hung over that grave like a pall,
But, borne on the breath of the last sad comer,
I listen again to the old-time call.

It is only a love of a by-gone season,
A senseless folly that mocked at me
A reckless passion that lacked all reason,
So I killed it, and hid it where none could see.

I smothered it first to stop its crying,
Then stabbed it through with a good sharp blade,
And cold and pallid I saw it lying,
And deep—ah' deep was the grave I made.

But now I know that there is no killing
A thing like Love, for it laughs at Death.
There is no hushing, there is no stilling
That which is part of your life and breath.

You may bury it deep, and leave behind you
The land, the people, that knew your slain;
It will push the sods from its grave, and find you
On wastes of water or desert plain.

You may hear but tongues of a foreign people,
You may list to sounds that are strange and new;
But, clear as a silver bell in a steeple,
That voice from the grave shall call to you.

You may rouse your pride, you may use your reason.
And seem for a space to slay Love so;
But, all in its own good time and season,
It will rise and follow wherever you go.

You shall sit sometimes, when the leaves are falling,
Alone with your heart, as I sit to-day,
And hear that voice from your dead Past calling
Out of the graves that you hid away.

A WALTZ-QUADRILLE

The band was playing a waltz-quadrille,
I felt as light as a wind-blown feather,
As we floated away, at the caller's will,
Through the intricate, mazy dance together.
Like mimic armies our lines were meeting,
Slowly advancing, and then retreating,
All decked in their bright array;
And back and forth to the music's rhyme
We moved together, and all the time
I knew you were going away.

The fold of your strong arm sent a thrill
From heart to brain as we gently glided
Like leaves on the wave of that waltz-quadrille;
Parted, met, and again divided—
You drifting one way, and I another,
Then suddenly turning and facing each other,
Then off in the blithe chasse,
Then airily back to our places swaying,
While every beat of the music seemed saying
That you were going away.

I said to my heart, "Let us take our fill
Of mirth and music and love and laughter;
For it all must end with this waltz-quadrille,
And life will be never the same life after.
Oh, that the caller might go on calling,
Oh, that the music might go on falling
Like a shower of silver spray,
While we whirled on to the vast Forever,
Where no hearts break, and no ties sever,
And no one goes away."

A clamor, a crash, and the band was still;
'Twas the end of the dream, and the end of the measure:
The last low notes of that waltz-quadrille
Seemed like a dirge o'er the death of Pleasure.
You said good-night, and the spell was over—
Too warm for a friend, and too cold for a lover—
There was nothing else to say;
But the lights looked dim, and the dancers weary,
And the music was sad, and the hall was dreary,
After you went away.

BEPPO

Why art thou sad, my Beppo? But last eve,
Here at my feet, thy dear head on my breast,
I heard thee say thy heart would no more grieve
Or feel the olden ennui and unrest.

What troubles thee? Am I not all thine own?—
I, so long sought, so sighed for and so dear?
And do I not live but for thee alone?
"Thou hast seen Lippo, whom I loved last year!"

Well, what of that? Last year is naught to me—
'Tis swallowed in the ocean of the past.
Art thou not glad 'twas Lippo, and not thee,
Whose brief bright day in that great gulf was cast.
Thy day is all before thee. Let no cloud,
Here in the very morn of our delight,
Drift up from distant foreign skies, to shroud
Our sun of love whose radiance is so bright.

"Thou art not first?" Nay, and he who would be
Defeats his own heart's dearest purpose then.
No truer truth was ever told to thee—
Who has loved most, he best can love again.

If Lippo (and not he alone) has taught
The arts that please thee, wherefore art thou sad?
Since all my vast love-lore to thee is brought,
Look up and smile, my Beppo, and be glad.

TIRED

I am tired to-night, and something,
The wind maybe, or the rain,
Or the cry of a bird in the copse outside,
Has brought back the past and its pain.
And I feel, as I sit here thinking,
That the hand of a dead old June
Has reached out hold of my heart's loose strings,
And is drawing them up in tune.

I am tired to-night, and I miss you,
And long for you, love, through tears;
And it seems but to-day that I saw you go—
You, who have been gone for years.
And I seem to be newly lonely—
I, who am so much alone;
And the strings of my heart are well in tune,
But they have not the same old tone.

I am tired; and that old sorrow
Sweeps down the bed of my soul,
As a turbulent river might sudden'y break
way from a dam's control.
It beareth a wreck on its bosom,
A wreck with a snow-white sail;
And the hand on my heart strings thrums away,
But they only respond with a wail.

THE SPEECH OF SILENCE

The solemn Sea of Silence lies between us;
I know thou livest, and them lovest me,
And yet I wish some white ship would come sailing
Across the ocean, beating word from thee.

The dead calm awes me with its awful stillness.
No anxious doubts or fears disturb my breast;
I only ask some little wave of language,
To stir this vast infinitude of rest.

I am oppressed with this great sense of loving;
So much I give, so much receive from thee;
Like subtle incense, rising from a censer,
So floats the fragrance of thy love round me.

All speech is poor, and written words unmeaning;
Yet such I ask, blown hither by some wind,
To give relief to this too perfect knowledge,
The Silence so impresses on my mind.

How poor the love that needeth word or message,
To banish doubt or nourish tenderness!
I ask them but to temper love's convictions
The Silence all too fully doth express.

Too deep the language which the spirit utters;
Too vast the knowledge which my soul hath stirred.
Send some white ship across the Sea of Silence,
And interrupt its utterance with a word.

CONVERSION

I have lived this life as the skeptic lives it;
I have said the sweetness was less than the gall;
Praising, nor cursing, the Hand that gives it,
I have drifted aimlessly through it all.
I have scoffed at the tale of a so-called heaven;
I have laughed at the thought of a Supreme Friend;
I have said that it only to man was given
To live, to endure; and to die was the end.

But I know that a good God reigneth,
Generous-hearted and kind and true;
Since unto a worm like me he deigneth
To send so royal a gift as you.
Bright as a star you gleam on my bosom,
Sweet as a rose that the wild bee sips;
And I know, my own, my beautiful blossom,
That none but a God could mould such lips.

And I believe, in the fullest measure
That ever a strong man's heart could hold,
In all the tales of heavenly pleasure
By poets sung or by prophets told;
For in the joy of your shy, sweet kisses,
Your pulsing touch and your languid sigh
I am filled and thrilled with better blisses
Than ever were claimed for souls on high.

And now I have faith in all the stories
Told of the beauties of unseen lands;
Of royal splendors and marvellous glories
Of the golden city not made with hands
For the silken beauty of falling tresses,
Of lips all dewy and cheeks aglow,

With—what the mind in a half trance guesses
Of the twin perfection of drifts of snow;

Of limbs like marble, of thigh and shoulder
Carved like a statue in high relief—
These, as the eyes and the thoughts grow bolder,
Leave no room for an unbelief.
So my lady, my queen most royal,
My skepticism has passed away;
If you are true to me, true and loyal,
I will believe till the Judgment-day.

LOVE'S COMING

She had looked for his coming as warriors come,
With the clash of arms and the bugle's call:
But he came instead with a stealthy tread,
Which she did not hear at all.

She had thought how his armor would blaze in the sun,
As he rode like a prince to claim his bride:
In the sweet dim light of the falling night
She found him at her side.

She had dreamed how the gaze of his strange, bold eye
Would wake her heart to a sudden glow:
She found in his face the familiar grace
Of a friend she used to know.

She had dreamed how his coming would stir her soul,
As the ocean is stirred by the wild storm's strife:
He brought her the balm of a heavenly calm,
And a peace which crowned her life.

OLD AND NEW

Long have the poets vaunted, in their lays,
Old times, old loves, old friendship, and old wine.
Why should the old monopolize all praise?
Then let the new claim mine.

Give me strong new friends when the old prove weak
Or fail me in my darkest hour of need;
Why perish with the ship that springs a leak
Or lean upon a reed?

Give me new love, warm, palpitating, sweet,
When all the grace and beauty leave the old;
When like a rose it withers at my feet,
Or like a hearth grows cold.

Give me new times, bright with a prosperous cheer,
In place of old, tear-blotted, burdened days;
I hold a sunlit present far more dear,
And worthy of my praise.

When the old deeds are threadbare and worn through,
And all too narrow for the broadening soul,
Give me the fine, firm texture of the new,
Fair, beautiful, and whole!

PERFECTNESS

All perfect things are saddening in effect.
The autumn wood robed in its scarlet clothes,
The matchless tinting on the royal rose
Whose velvet leaf by no least flaw is flecked,
Love's supreme moment, when the soul unchecked
Soars high as heaven, and its best rapture knows—
These hold a deeper pathos than our woes,
Since they leave nothing better to expect.

Resistless change, when powerless to improve,
Can only mar. The gold will pale to gray;
Nothing remains tomorrow as to-day;
The lose will not seem quite so fait, and love
Must find its measures of delight made less.
Ah, how imperfect is all Perfectness!

ATTRACTION

The meadow and the mountain with desire
Gazed on each other, till a fierce unrest
Surged 'neath the meadow's seemingly calm breast,
And all the mountain's fissures ran with fire.

A mighty river rolled between them there.
What could the mountain do but gaze and burn?
What could the meadow do but look and yearn,
And gem its bosom to conceal despair?

Their seething passion agitated space,
Till, lo! the lands a sudden earthquake shook,
The river fled, the meadow leaped and took
The leaning mountain in a close embrace.

GRACIA

Nay, nay, Antonio! nay, thou shalt not blame her,
My Gracia, who hath so deserted me.
Thou art my friend, but if thou dost defame her
I shall not hesitate to challenge thee.

"Curse and forget her?" So I might another,
One not so bounteous-natured or so fair;
But she, Antonio, she was like no other—
I curse her not, because she was so rare.

She was made out of laughter and sweet kisses;
Not blood, but sunshine, through her blue veins ran
Her soul spilled over with its wealth of blisses;
She was too great for loving but a man.

None but a god could keep so rare a creature:
I blame her not for her inconstancy;
When I recall each radiant smile and feature,
I wonder she so long was true to me.

Call her not false or fickle. I, who love her,
Do hold her not unlike the royal sun,
That, all unmated, roams the wide world over
And lights all worlds, but lingers not with one.

If she were less a goddess, more a woman,
And so had dallied for a time with me,
And then had left me, I, who am but human,
Would slay her and her newer love, maybe.

But since she seeks Apollo, or another
Of those lost gods (and seeks him all in vain)
And has loved me as well as any other
Of her men loves, why, I do not complain.

AD FINEM

On the white throat of the' useless passion
That scorched my soul with its burning breath
I clutched my fingers in murderous fashion,
And gathered them close in a grip of death;
For why should I fan, or feed with fuel,
A love that showed me but blank despair?
So my hold was firm, and my grasp was cruel—
I meant to strangle it then and there!

I thought it was dead. But with no warning,
It rose from its grave last night, and came
And stood by my bed till the early morning,
And over and over it spoke your name.
Its throat was red where my hands had held it;
It burned my brow with its scorching breath;
And I said, the moment my eyes beheld it,
"A love like this can know no death."

For just one kiss that your lips have given
In the lost and beautiful past to me
I would gladly barter my hopes of Heaven
And all the bliss of Eternity.
For never a joy are the angels keeping,
To lay at my feet in Paradise,
Like that of into your strong arms creeping,
And looking into your love-lit eyes.

I know, in the way that sins are reckoned,
This thought is a sin of the deepest dye;
But I know, too, if an angel beckoned,
Standing close by the Throne on High,
And you, adown by the gates infernal,
Should open your loving arms and smile,

I would turn my back on things supernal,
To lie on your breast a little while.

To know for an hour you were mine completely—
Mine in body and soul, my own—
I would bear unending tortures sweetly,
With not a murmur and not a moan.
A lighter sin or a lesser error
Might change through hope or fear divine;
But there is no fear, and hell has no terror,
To change or alter a love like mine.

BLEAK WEATHER

Dear Love, where the red lilies blossomed and grew
The white snows are falling;
And all through the woods where I wandered with you
The loud winds are calling;
And the robin that piped to us tune upon tune,
Neath the oak, you remember,
O'er hill-top and forest has followed the June
And left us December.

He has left like a friend who is true in the sun
And false in the shadows;
He has found new delights in the land where he's gone,
Greener woodlands and meadows.
Let him go! what care we? let the snow shroud the lea,
Let it drift on the heather;
We can sing through it all: I have you, you have me.
And we'll laugh at the weather.

The old year may die and a new year be born
That is bleaker and colder:
It cannot dismay us; we dare it, we scorn,
For our love makes us bolder.
Ah, Robin! sing loud on your far distant lea,
You friend in fair weather!
But here is a song sung that's fuller of glee,
By two warm hearts together.

AN ANSWER

If all the year was summer time,
And all the aim of life
Was just to lilt on like a rhyme,
Then I would be your wife.

If all the days were August days,
And crowned with golden weather,
How happy then through green-clad ways
We two could stray together!

If all the nights were moonlit nights,
And we had naught to do
But just to sit and plan delights,
Then I would wed with you.

If life was all a summer fete,
Its soberest pace the "glide,"
Then I would choose you for my mate,
And keep you at my side.

But winter makes full half the year,
And labor half of life,
And all the laughter and good cheer
Give place to wearing strife.

Days will grow cold, and moons wax old.
And then a heart that's true
Is better far than grace or gold—
And so, my love, adieu!
I cannot wed with you.

YOU WILL FORGET ME

You will forget me. The years are so tender,
They bind up the wounds which we think are so deep;
This dream of our youth will fade out as the splendor
Fades from the skies when the sun sinks to sleep;
The cloud of forgetfulness, over and over
Will banish the last rosy colors away,
And the fingers of time will weave garlands to cover
The scar which you think is a life-mark to-day.

You will forget me. The one boon you covet
Now above all things will soon seem no prize;
And the heart, which you hold not in keeping to prove it
True or untrue, will lose worth in your eyes.
The one drop to-day, that you deem only wanting
To fill your life-cup to the brim, soon will seem
But a valueless mite; and the ghost that is haunting
The aisles of your heart will pass out with the dream.

You will forget me; will thank me for saying
The words which you think are so pointed with pain.
Time loves a new lay; and the dirge he is playing
Will change for you soon to a livelier strain.
I shall pass from your life—I shall pass out forever,
And these hours we have spent will be sunk in the past.
Youth buries its dead; grief kills seldom or never,
And forgetfulness covers all sorrows at last.

THE FAREWELL OF CLARIMONDE

(Suggested by the "Clarimonde" Of Théophile Gautier.)

Adieu, Romauld! But thou canst not forget me.
Although no more I haunt thy dreams at night,
Thy hungering heart forever must regret me,
And starve for those lost moments of delight.

Naught shall avail thy priestly rites and duties,
Nor fears of Hell, nor hopes of Heaven beyond:
Before the Cross shall rise my fair form's beauties—-
The lips, the limbs, the eyes of Clarimonde.

Like gall the wine sipped from the sacred chalice
Shall taste to one who knew my red mouth's bliss,
When Youth and Beauty dwelt in Love's own palace,
And life flowed on in one eternal kiss.

Through what strange ways I come, dear heart, to reach thee,
From viewless lands, by paths no man e'er trod!
I braved all fears, all dangers dared, to teach thee
A love more mighty than thy love of God.

Think not in all His Kingdom to discover
Such joys, Romauld, as ours, when fierce yet fond
I clasped thee—kissed thee—crowned thee my one lover:
Thou canst not find another Clarimonde.

I knew all arts of love: he who possessed me
Possessed all women, and could never tire;
A new life dawned for him who once caressed me;
Satiety itself I set on fire.

Inconstancy I chained: men died to win me;
Kings cast by crowns for one hour on my breast:
And all the passionate tide of love within me
I gave to thee, Romauld. Wert thou not blest?

Yet, for the love of God, thy hand hath riven
Our welded souls. But not in prayer well conned,
Not in thy dearly-purchased peace of Heaven,
Canst thou forget those hours with Clarimonde.

THE TRIO

We love but once. The great gold orb of light
From dawn to even-tide doth cast his ray;
But the full splendor of his perfect might
Is reached but once throughout the livelong day.

We love but once. The waves, with ceaseless motion,
Do day and night plash on the pebbled shore;
But the strong tide of the resistless ocean
Sweeps in but one hour of the twenty-four.

We love but once. A score of times, perchance,
We may be moved in fancy's fleeting fashion—
May treasure up a word, a tone, a glance;
But only once we feel the soul's great passion.

We love but once. Love walks with death and birth
(The saddest, the unkindest of the three);
And only once while we sojourn on earth
Can that strange trio come to you or me.

MISCELLANEOUS POEMS

THE LOST GARDEN

There was a fair green garden sloping
From the south-east side of the mountain-ledge;
And the earliest tint of the dawn came groping
Down through its paths, from the day's dim edge.
The bluest skies and the reddest roses
Arched and varied its velvet sod;
And the glad birds sang, as the soul supposes
The angels sing on the hills of God.

I wandered there when my veins seemed bursting
With life's rare rapture and keen delight,
And yet in my heart was a constant thirsting
For something over the mountain-height.
I wanted to stand in the blaze of glory
That turned to crimson the peaks of snow,
And the winds from the west all breathed a story
Of realms and regions I longed to know.

I saw on the garden's south side growing
The brightest blossoms that breathe of June;
I saw in the east how the sun was glowing,
And the gold air shook with a wild bird's tune;
I heard the drip of a silver fountain,
And the pulse of a young laugh throbbed with glee

But still I looked out over the mountain
Where unnamed wonders awaited me.

I came at last to the western gateway,
That led to the path I longed to climb;
But a shadow fell on my spirit straightway,
For close at my side stood gray-beard Time.
I paused, with feet that were fain to linger,
Hard by that garden's golden gate,
But Time spoke, pointing with one stern finger;
"Pass on," he said, "for the day groes late."

And now on the chill giay cliffs I wander,
The heights recede which I thought to find,
And the light seems dim on the mountain yonder,
When I think of the garden I left behind.
Should I stand at last on its summit's splendor,
I know full well it would not repay
For the fair lost tints of the dawn so tender
That crept up over the edge o' day.

I would go back, but the ways are winding,
If ways there are to that land, in sooth,
For what man succeeds in ever finding
A path to the garden of his lost youth?
But I think sometimes, when the June stars glisten,
That a rose scent dufts from far away,
And I know, when I lean from the cliffs and listen,
That a young laugh breaks on the air like spray.

ART AND HEART

Though critics may bow to art, and I am its own true lover,
It is not art, but *heart*, which wins the wide world over.

Though smooth be the heartless prayer, no ear in Heaven will
mind it,
And the finest phrase falls dead if there is no feeling behind it.

Though perfect the player's touch, little, if any, he sways us,
Unless we feel his heart throb through the music he plays us.

Though the poet may spend his life in skilfully rounding a
measure,
Unless he writes from a full, warm heart he gives us little
pleasure.

So it is not the speech which tells, but the impulse which goes
with the saying;
And it is not the words of the prayer, but the yearning back of
the praying.

It is not the artist's skill which into our soul comes stealing
With a joy that is almost pain, but it is the player's feeling.

And it is not the poet's song, though sweeter than sweet bells
chiming,
Which thrills us through and through, but the heart which
beats under the rhyming.

And therefore I say again, though I am art's own true lover,
That it is not art, but heart, which wins the wide world over.

MOCKERY

Why do we grudge our sweets so to the living
Who, God knows, find at best too much of gall,
And then with generous, open hands kneel, giving
Unto the dead our all?

Why do we pierce the warm hearts, sin or sorrow,
With idle jests, or scorn, or cruel sneers,
And when it cannot know, on some to-morrow,
Speak of its woe through tears?

What do the dead care, for the tender token—
The love, the praise, the floral offerings?
But palpitating, living hearts are broken
For want of just these things.

AS BY FIRE

Sometimes I feel so passionate a yearning
For spiritual perfection here below,
This vigorous frame, with healthful fervor burning,
Seems my determined foe,

So actively it makes a stern resistance,
So cruelly sometimes it wages war
Against a wholly spiritual existence
Which I am striving for.

It interrupts my soul's intense devotions;
Some hope it strangles, of divinest birth,
With a swift rush of violent emotions
Which link me to the earth.

It is as if two mortal foes contended
Within my bosom in a deadly strife,
One for the loftier aims for souls intended,
One for the earthly life.

And yet I know this very war within me,
Which brings out all my will-power and control,
This very conflict at the last shall win me
The loved and longed-for goal.

The very fire which seems sometimes so cruel
Is the white light that shows me my own strength.
A furnace, fed by the divinest fuel,
It may become at length.

Ah! when in the immortal ranks enlisted,
I sometimes wonder if we shall not find
That not by deeds, but by what we've resisted,
Our places are assigned.

IF I SHOULD DIE

RONDEAU

If I should die, how kind you all would grow!
In that strange hour I would not have one foe.
There are no words too beautiful to say
Of one who goes forevermore away
Across that ebbing tide which has no flow.

With what new lustre my good deeds would glow!
If faults were mine, no one would call them so,
Or speak of me in aught but praise that day,
If I should die.

Ah, friends! before my listening ear lies low,
While I can hear and understand, bestow
That gentle treatment and fond love, I pray,
The lustre of whose late though radiant way
Would gild my grave with mocking light, I know,
If I should die.

MÉSALLIANCE

I am troubled to-night with a curious pain;
It is not of the flesh, it is not of the brain,
Nor yet of a heart that is breaking:
But down still deeper, and out of sight—
In the place where the soul and the body unite—
There lies the scat of the aching.

They have been lovers in days gone by;
But the soul is fickle, and longs to fly
From the fettering mesalliance:
And she tears at the bonds which are binding her so,
And pleads with the body to let her go,
But he will not yield compliance.

For the body loves, as he loved in the past,
When he wedded the soul; and he holds her fast,
And swears that he will not loose her;
That he will keep her and hide her away
For ever and ever and for a day
From the arms of Death, the seducer.

Ah! this is the strife that is wearying me—
The strife 'twixt a soul that would be free
And a body that will not let her.
And I say to my soul, "Be calm, and wait;
For I tell ye truly that soon or late
Ye surely shall drop each fetter."

And I say to the body, "Be kind, I pray;
For the soul is not of thy mortal clay,
But is formed in spirit fashion."
And still through the hours of the solemn night
I can hear my sad soul's plea for flight,
And my body's reply of passion.

RESPONSE

I said this morning, as I leaned and threw
My shutters open to the Spring's surprise,
"Tell me, O Earth, how is it that in you
Year after year the same fresh feelings rise?
How do you keep your young exultant glee?
No more those sweet emotions come to me.

"I note through all your fissures how the tide
Of healthful life goes leaping as of old;
Your royal dawns retain their pomp and pride;
Your sunsets lose no atom of their gold.
How can this wonder be?" My soul's fine ear
Leaned, listening, till a small voice answered near:

"My days lapse never over into night;
My nights encroach not on the rights of dawn.
I rush not breathless after some delight;
I waste no grief for any pleasure gone.
My July noons burn not the entire year.
Heart, hearken well!" "Yes, yes; go on; I hear."

"I do not strive to make my sunsets' gold
Pave all the dim and distant realms of space.
I do not bid my crimson dawns unfold
To lend the midnight a fictitious grace.
I break no law, for all God's laws are good.
Heart, hast thou heard?" "Yes, yes; and understood."

DROUTH

Why do we pity those who weep? The pain
That finds a ready outlet in the flow
Of salt and bitter tears is blessed woe,
And does not need our sympathies. The rain
But fits the shorn field for new yield of grain;
While the red, brazen skies, the sun's fierce glow,
The dry, hot winds that from the tropics blow
Do parch and wither the unsheltered plain.
The anguish that through long, remorseless years
Looks out upon the world with no relief
Of sudden tempests or slow-dripping tears—
The still, unuttered, silent, wordless grief
That evermore doth ache, and ache, and ache—
This is the sorrow wherewith hearts do break.

THE CREED

Whoever was begotten by pure love,
And came desired and welcome into life,
Is of immaculate conception. He
Whose heart is full of tenderness and truth,
Who loves mankind more than he loves himself,
And cannot find room in his heart for hate,
May be another Christ. We all may be
The Saviours of the world if we believe
In the Divinity which dwells in us
And worship it, and nail our grosser selves,
Our tempers, greeds, and our unworthy aims,
Upon the cross. Who giveth love to all;
Pays kindness for unkindness, smiles for frowns;
And lends new courage to each fainting heart,
And strengthens hope and scatters joy abroad—
He, too, is a Redeemer, Son of God.

PROGRESS

Let there be many windows to your soul,
That all the glory of the universe
May beautify it. Not the narrow pane
Of one poor creed can catch the radiant rays
That shine from countless sources. Tear away
The blinds of superstition; let the light
Pour through fair windows broad as Truth itself
And high as God.

Why should the spirit peer
Through some priest-curtained orifice, and grope
Along dim corridors of doubt, when all
The splendor from unfathomed seas of space
Might bathe it with the golden waves of Love?
Sweep up the debris of decaying faiths;
Sweep down the cobwebs of worn-out beliefs,
And throw your soul wide open to the light
Of Reason and of Knowledge. Tune your ear
To all the wordless music of the stars
And to the voice of Nature, and your heart
Shall turn to truth and goodness as the plant
Turns to the sun. A thousand unseen hands
Reach down to help you to their peace-crowned heights.
And all the forces of the firmament
Shall fortify your strength. Be not afraid
To thrust aside half-truths and grasp the whole.

MY FRIEND

When first I looked upon the face of Pain
I shrank repelled, as one shrinks from a foe
Who stands with dagger poised, as for a blow.
I was in search of Pleasure and of Gain;
I turned aside to let him pass: in vain;
He looked straight in my eyes and would not go.
"Shake hands," he said; "our paths are one, and so
We must be comrades on the way, 'tis plain."

I felt the firm clasp of his hand on mine;
Through all my veins it sent a strengthening glow.
I straightway linked my arm in his, and lo!
He led me forth to joys almost divine;
With God's great truths enriched me in the end:
And now I hold him as my dearest friend.

CREATION

The impulse of all love is to create.
God was so full of love, in his embrace
He clasped the empty nothingness of space,
And low! the solar system! High in state
The mighty sun sat, so supreme and great
With this same essence, one smile of its face
Brought myriad forms of life forth; race on race,
From insects up to men.

Through love, not hate,
All that is grand in nature or in art
Sprang into being. He who would build sublime
And lasting works, to stand the test of time,
Must inspiration draw from his full heart.
And he who loveth widely, well, and much,
The secret holds of the true master touch.

RED CARNATIONS

One time in Arcadie's fair bowers
There met a bright immortal band,
To choose their emblems from the flowers
That made an Eden of that land.

Sweet Constancy, with eyes of hope,
Strayed down the garden path alone
And gathered sprays of heliotrope,
To place in clusters at her zone.

True Friendship plucked the ivy green,
Forever fresh, forever fair.
Inconstancy with flippant mien
The fading primrose chose to wear.

One moment Love the rose paused by;
But Beauty picked it for her hair.
Love paced the garden with a sigh
He found no fitting emblem there.

Then suddenly he saw a flame,
A conflagration turned to bloom;
It even put the rose to shame,
Both in its beauty and perfume.

He watched it, and it did not fade;
He plucked it, and it brighter grew.
In cold or heat, all undismayed,
It kept its fragrance and its hue.

"Here deathless love and passion sleep,"
He cried, "embodied in this flower.
This is the emblem I will keep."
Love wore carnations from that hour.

LIFE IS TOO SHORT

Life is too short for any vain regretting;
Let dead delight bury its dead, I say,
And let us go upon our way forgetting
The joys and sorrows of each yesterday
Between the swift sun's rising and its setting
We have no time for useless tears or fretting:
Life is too short.

Life is too short for any bitter feeling;
Time is the best avenger if we wait;
The years speed by, and on their wings bear healing;
We have no room for anything like hate.
This solemn truth the low mounds seem revealing
That thick and fast about our feet are stealing:
Life is too short.

Life is too short for aught but high endeavor—
Too short for spite, but long enough for love.
And love lives on forever and forever;
It links the worlds that circle on above:
'Tis God's first law, the universe's lever.
In His vast realm the radiant souls sigh never
"Life is too short."

A SCULPTOR

As the ambitious sculptor, tireless, lifts
Chisel and hammer to the block at hand,
Before my half-formed character I stand
And ply the shining tools of mental gifts.
I'll cut away a huge, unsightly side
Of selfishness, and smooth to curves of grace
The angles of ill-temper.

And no trace
Shall my sure hammer leave of silly pride.
Chip after chip must fall from vain desires,
And the sharp corners of my discontent
Be rounded into symmetry, and lent
Great harmony by faith that never tires.
Unfinished still, I must toil on and on,
Till the pale critic, Death, shall say, "'Tis done."

BEYOND

It seemeth such a little way to me
Across to that strange country—the Beyond;
And yet, not strange, for it has grown to be
The home of those of whom I am so fond,
They make it seem familiar and most dear,
As journeying friends bring distant regions near.

So close it lies that when my sight is clear
I think I almost see the gleaming strand.
I know I feel those who have gone from here
Come near enough sometimes to touch my hand.
I often think, but for our veiled eyes,
We should find Heaven right round about us lies.

I cannot make it seem a day to dread,
When from this dear earth I shall journey out
To that still dearer country of the dead,
And join the lost ones, so long dreamed about.
I love this world, yet shall I love to go
And meet the friends who wait for me, I know.

I never stand above a bier and see
The seal of death set on some well-loved face
But that I think, "One more to welcome me
When I shall cross the intervening space
Between this land and that one 'over there';
One more to make the strange Beyond seem fair."

And so for me there is no sting to death,
And so the grave has lost its victory.
It is but crossing—with a bated breath
And white, set face—a little strip of sea
To find the loved ones waiting on the shore,
More beautiful, more precious than before.

THE SADDEST HOUR

The saddest hour of anguish and of loss
Is not that season of supreme despair
When we can find no least light anywhere
To gild the dread, black shadow of the Cross;
Not in that luxury of sorrow when
We sup on salt of tears, and drink the gall
Of memories of days beyond recall—
Of lost delights that cannot come again.

But when, with eyes that are no longer wet,
We look out on the great, wide world of men,
And, smiling, lean toward a bright to-morrow,
Then backward shrink, with sudden keen regret,
To find that we are learning to forget:
Ah! then we face the saddest hour of sorrow.

SHOW ME THE WAY

Show me the way that leads to the true life.
I do not care what tempests may assail me,
I shall be given courage for the strife;
I know my strength will not desert or fail me;
I know that I shall conquer in the fray:
Show me the way.

Show me the way up to a higher plane,
Where body shall be servant to the soul.
I do not care what tides of woe or pain
Across my life their angry waves may roll,
If I but reach the end I seek, some day:
Show me the way.

Show me the way, and let me bravely climb
Above vain grievings for unworthy treasures;
Above all sorrow that finds balm in time;
Above small triumphs or belittling pleasures;
Up to those heights where these things seem child's-play:
Show me the way.

Show me the way to that calm, perfect peace
Which springs from an inward consciousness of right;
To where all conflicts with the flesh shall cease,
And self shall radiate with the spirit's light.
Though hard the journey and the strife, I pray,
Show me the way.

MY HERITAGE

I into life so full of love was sent
That all the shadows which fall on the way
Of every human being could not stay,
But fled before the light my spirit lent.

I saw the world through gold and crimson dyes:
Men sighed and said, "Those rosy hues will fade
As you pass on into the glare and shade!"
Still beautiful the way seems to mine eyes.

They said, "You are too jubilant and glad;
The world is full of sorrow and of wrong.
Full soon your lips shall breathe forth sighs—not song."
The day wears on, and yet I am not sad.

They said, "You love too largely, and you must,
Through wound on wound, grow bitter to your kind."
They were false prophets; day by day I find
More cause for love, and less cause for distrust.

They said, "Too free you give your soul's rare wine;
The world will quaff, but it will not repay."
Yet in the emptied flagons, day by day,
True hearts pour back a nectar as divine.

Thy heritage! Is it not love's estate?
Look to it, then, and keep its soil well tilled.
I hold that my best wishes are fulfilled
Because I love so much, and cannot hate.

RESOLVE

Build on resolve, and not upon regret,
The structure of thy future. Do not grope
Among the shadows of old sins, but let
Thine own soul's light shine on the path of hope
And dissipate the darkness. Waste no tears
Upon the blotted record of lost years,
But turn the leaf and smile, oh, smile, to see
The fair white pages that remain for thee.

Prate not of thy repentance. But believe
The spark divine dwells in thee: let it grow.
That which the upreaching spirit can achieve
The grand and all-creative forces know;
They will assist and strengthen as the light
Lifts up the acorn to the oak tree's height.
Thou hast but to resolve, and lo! God's whole
Great universe shall fortify thy soul.

AT ELEUSIS

I, at Eleusis, saw the finest sight,
When early morning's banners were unfurled.
From high Olympus, gazing on the world,
The ancient gods once saw it with delight.
Sad Demeter had in a single night
Removed her sombre garments! and mine eyes
Beheld a 'broidered mantle in pale dyes
Thrown o'er her throbbing bosom. Sweet and clear
There fell the sound of music on mine ear.
And from the South came Hermes, he whose lyre
One time appeased the great Apollo's ire.
The rescued maid, Persephone, by the hand
He led to waiting Demeter, and cheer
And light and beauty once more blessed the land.

COURAGE

There is a courage, a majestic thing
That springs forth from the brow of pain, full-grown,
Minerva-like, and dares all dangers known,
And all the threatening future yet may bring;
Crowned with the helmet of great suffering;
Serene with that grand strength by martyrs shown,
When at the stake they die and make no moan,
And even as the flames leap up are heard to sing:

A courage so sublime and unafraid,
It wears its sorrows like a coat of mail;
And Fate, the archer, passes by dismayed,
Knowing his best barbed arrows needs must fail
To pierce a soul so armored and arrayed
That Death himself might look on it and quail.

SOLITUDE

Laugh, and the world laughs with you;
Weep, and you weep alone;
For the sad old earth must borrow its mirth,
But has trouble enough of its own.
Sing, and the hills will answer;
Sigh, it is lost on the air;
The echoes bound to a joyful sound,
But shrink from voicing care.

Rejoice, and men will seek you;
Grieve, and they turn and go;
They want full measure of all your pleasure,
But they do not need your woe.
Be glad, and your friends are many;
Be sad, and you lose them all;
There are none to decline your nectar'd wine,
But alone you must drink life's gall.

Feast, and your halls are crowded;
Fast, and the world goes by.
Succeed and give, and it helps you live,
But no man can help you die.
There is room in the halls of pleasure
For a large and lordly train,
But one by one we must all file on
Through the narrow aisles of pain.

THE YEAR OUTGROWS THE SPRING

The year outgrows the spring it thought so sweet,
And clasps the summer with a new delight,
Yet wearied, leaves her languors and her heat
When cool-browed autumn dawns upon his sight.

The tree outgrows the bud's suggestive grace,
And feels new pride in blossoms fully blown.
But even this to deeper joy gives place
When bending boughs 'neath blushing burdens groan.

Life's rarest moments are derived from change.
The heart outgrows old happiness, old grief,
And suns itself in feelings new and strange;
The most enduring pleasure is but brief.

Our tastes, our needs, are never twice the same.
Nothing contents us long, however dear.
The spirit in us, like the grosser frame,
Outgrows the garments which it wore last year.

Change is the watchword of Progression. When
We tire of well-worn ways we seek for new.
This restless craving in the souls of men
Spurs them to climb, and seek the mountain view.

So let who will erect an altar shrine
To meek-browed Constancy, and sing her praise.
Unto enlivening Change I shall build mine,
Who lends new zest and interest to my days.

THE BEAUTIFUL LAND OF NOD

Come, cuddle your head on my shoulder, dear,
Your head like the golden-rod,
And we will go sailing away from here
To the beautiful Land of Nod.
Away from life's hurry and flurry and worry,
Away from earth's shadows and gloom,
To a world of fair weather we'll float off together,
Where roses are always in bloom.

Just shut your eyes and fold your hands,
Your hands like the leaves of a rose,
And we will go sailing to those fair lands
That never an atlas shows.
On the North and the West they are bounded by rest,
On the South and the East, by dreams;
'Tis the country ideal, where nothing is real,
But everything only seems.

Just drop down the curtains of your dear eyes
Those eyes like a bright bluebell,
And we will sail out under starlit skies,
To the land where the fairies dwell.

Down the river of sleep our barque shall sweep,
Till it reaches that mystical Isle
Which no man hath seen, but where all have been,
And there we will pause awhile.
I will croon you a song as we float along
To that shore that is blessed of God,
Then, ho! for that fair land, we're off for that rare land,
That beautiful Land of Nod.

THE TIGER

In the still jungle of the senses lay
A tiger soundly sleeping, till one day
A bold young hunter chanced to come that way.

"How calm," he said, "that splendid creature lies!
I long to rouse him into swift surprise."
The well aimed arrow shot from amorous eyes,

And lo! the tiger rouses up and turns,
A coal of fire his glowing eyeball burns,
His mighty frame with savage hunger yearns.

He crouches for a spring; his eyes dilate—
Alas! bold hunter, what shall be thy fate?
Thou canst not fly; it is too late, too late.

Once having tasted human flesh, ah! then,
Woe, woe unto the whole rash world of men.
The wakened tiger will not sleep again.

ONLY A SIMPLE RHYME

Only a simple rhyme of love and sorrow,
Where "blisses" rhymed with "kisses," "heart," with "dart:"
Yet, reading it, new strength I seemed to borrow,
To live on bravely and to do my part.

A little rhyme about a heart that's bleeding—
Of lonely hours and sorrow's unrelief:
I smiled at first; but there came with the reading
A sense of sweet companionship in grief.

The selfishness of my own woe forsaking,
I thought about the singer of that song.
Some other breast felt this same weary aching;
Another found the summer days too long.

The few sad lines, my sorrow so expressing,
I read, and on the singer, all unknown,
I breathed a fervent though a silent blessing,
And seemed to clasp his hand within my own.

And though fame pass him and he never know it,
And though he never sings another strain,
He has performed the mission of the poet,
In helping some sad heart to bear its pain.

I WILL BE WORTHY OF IT

I may not reach the heights I seek,
My untried strength may fail me,
Or, half-way up the mountain peak,
Fierce tempests may assail me.
But though that place I never gain,
Herein lies comfort for my pain—
I will be worthy of it.

I may not triumph in success,
Despite my earnest labor;
I may not grasp results that bless
The efforts of my neighbor;
But though my goal I never see,
This thought shall always dwell with me—
I will be worthy of it.

The golden glory of Love's light
May never fall on my way;
My path may always lead through night,
Like some deserted by-way;
But though life's dearest joy I miss
There lies a nameless strength in this—
I will be worthy of it.

SONNET

Methinks ofttimes my heart is like some bee
That goes forth through the summer day and sings.
And gathers honey from all growing things
In garden plot or on the clover lea.

When the long afternoon grows late, and she
Would seek her hive, she cannot lift her wings.
So heavily the too sweet bin den clings,
From which she would not, and yet would, fly free.

So with my full, fond heart; for when it tries
To lift itself to peace crowned heights, above
The common way where countless feet have trod,
Lo! then, this burden of dear human ties,
This growing weight of precious earthly love,
Binds down the spirit that would soar to God.

REGRET

There is a haunting phantom called Regret,
A shadowy creature robed somewhat like Woe,
But fairer in the face, whom all men know
By her sad mien and eyes forever wet.
No heart would seek her; but once having met,
All take her by the hand, and to and fro
They wander through those paths of long ago—
Those hallowed ways 'twere wiser to forget.

One day she led me to that lost land's gate
And bade me enter; but I answered "No!
I will pass on with my bold comrade, Fate;
I have no tears to waste on thee—no time;
My strength I hoard for heights I hope to climb:
No friend art thou for souls that would be great."

LET ME LEAN HARD

Let me lean hard upon the Eternal Breast:
In all earth's devious ways I sought for rest
And found it not. I will be strong, said I,
And lean upon myself. I will not cry
And importune all heaven with my complaint.
But now my strength fails, and I fall, I faint:
Let me lean hard.

Let me lean hard upon the unfailing Arm.
I said I will walk on, I fear no harm,
The spark divine within my soul will show
The upward pathway where my feet should go.
But now the heights to which I most aspire
Are lost in clouds. I stumble and I tire:
Let me lean hard.

Let me lean harder yet. That swerveless force
Which speeds the solar systems on their course
Can take, unfelt, the burden of my woe,
Which bears me to the dust and hurts me so.
I thought my strength enough for any fate,
But lo! I sink beneath my sorrow's weight:
Let me lean hard.

PENALTY

Because of the fullness of what I had
All that I have seems void and vain.
If I had not been happy I were not sad;
Though my salt is savorless, why complain?

From the ripe perfection of what was mine,
All that is mine seems worse than naught;
Yet I know as I sit in the dark and pine,
No cup could be drained which had not been fraught.

From the throb and thrill of a day that was,
The day that now is seems dull with gloom;
Yet I bear its dullness and darkness because
'Tis but the reaction of glow and bloom.

From the royal feast which of old was spread
I am starved on the diet which now is mine;
Yet I could not turn hungry from water and bread,
If I had not been sated on fruit and wine.

SUNSET

I saw the day lean o'er the world's sharp edge
And peer into night's chasm, dark and damp;
High in his hand he held a blazing lamp,
Then dropped it and plunged headlong down the ledge.

With lurid splendor that swift paled to gray,
I saw the dim skies suddenly flush bright.
'Twas but the expiring glory of the light
Flung from the hand of the adventurous day.

THE WHEEL OF THE BREAST

Through rivers of veins on the nameless quest
The tide of my life goes hurriedly sweeping,
Till it reaches that curious wheel o' the breast,
The human heart, which is never at rest.
Faster, faster, it cries, and leaping,
Plunging, dashing, speeding away,
The wheel and the river work night and day.

I know not wherefore, I know not whither,
This strange tide rushes with such mad force:
It glides on hither, it slides on thither,
Over and over the selfsame course,
With never an outlet and never a source;
And it lashes itself to the heat of passion
And whirls the heart in a mill-wheel fashion.

I can hear in the hush of the still, still night,
The ceaseless sound of that mighty river;
I can hear it gushing, gurgling, rushing,
With a wild, delirious, strange delight,
And a conscious pride in its sense of might,
As it hurries and worries my heart forever.

And I wonder oft as I lie awake,
And list to the river that seethes and surges
Over the wheel that it chides and urges—
I wonder oft if that wheel will break
With the mighty pressure it bears, some day,
Or slowly and wearily wear away.

For little by little the heart is wearing,
Like the wheel of the mill, as the tide goes tearing
And plunging hurriedly through my breast,
In a network of veins on a nameless quest,

From and forth, unto unknown oceans,
Bringing its cargoes of fierce emotions,
With never a pause or an hour for rest.

A MEETING

Quite carelessly I turned the newsy sheet;
A song I sang, full many a year ago,
Smiled up at me, as in a busy street
One meets an old-time friend he used to know.

So full it was, that simple little song,
Of all the hope, the transport, and the truth,
Which to the impetuous morn of life belong,
That once again I seemed to grasp my youth.

So full it was of that sweet, fancied pain
We woo and cherish ere we meet with woe,
I felt as one who hears a plaintive strain
His mother sang him in the long ago.

Up from the grave the years that lay between
That song's birthday and my stern present came
Like phantom forms and swept across the scene,
Bearing their broken dreams of love and fame.

Fair hopes and bright ambitions that I knew
In that old time, with their ideal grace,
Shone for a moment, then were lost to view
Behind the dull clouds of the commonplace.

With trembling hands I put the sheet away;
Ah, little song! the sad and bitter truth
Struck like an arrow when we met that day!
My life has missed the promise of its youth.

EARNESTNESS

The hurry of the times affects us so
In this swift rushing hour, we crowd and press
And thrust each other backward as we go,
And do not pause to lay sufficient stress
Upon that good, strong, true word, Earnestness.
In our impetuous haste, could we but know
Its full, deep meaning, its vast import, oh,
Then might we grasp the secret of success!
In that receding age when men were great,
The bone and sinew of their purpose lay
In this one word. God likes an earnest soul—
Too earnest to be eager. Soon or late
It leaves the spent horde breathless by the way,
And stands serene, triumphant at the goal.

A PICTURE

I strolled last eve across the lonely down;
One solitary picture struck my eye:
A distant ploughboy stood against the sky—
How far he seemed above the noisy town!

Upon the bosom of a cloud the sod
Laid its bruised cheek as he moved slowly by,
And, watching him, I asked myself if I
In very truth stood half as near to God.

TWIN-BORN

He who possesses virtue at its best,
Or greatness in the true sense of the word,
Has one day started even with that herd
Whose swift feet now speed but at sin's behest.
It is the same force in the human breast
Which makes men gods or demons. If we gird
Those strong emotions by which we are stirred
With might of will and purpose, heights unguessed
Shall dawn for us; or if we give them sway
We can sink down and consort with the lost.
All virtue is worth just the price it cost.
Black sin is oft white truth that missed its way
And wandered off in paths not understood.
Twin-born I hold great evil and great good.

FLOODS

In the dark night, from sweet refreshing sleep
I wake to hear outside my window-pane
The uncurbed fury of the wild spring rain,
And weird winds lashing the defiant deep,
And roar of floods that gather strength and leap
Down dizzy, wreck-strewn channels to the main.
I turn upon my pillow and again
Compose myself for slumber.
Let them sweep;
I once survived great floods, and do not fear,
Though ominous planets congregate, and seem
To foretell strange disasters.
From a dream—
Ah! dear God! such a dream!—I woke to hear,
Through the dense shadows lit by no star's gleam,
The rush of mighty waters on my ear.
Helpless, afraid, and all alone, I lay;
The floods had come upon me unaware.
I heard the crash of structures that were fair;
The bridges of fond hopes were swept away
By great salt waves of sorrow. In dismay
I saw by the red lightning's lurid glare
That on the rock-bound island of despair
I had been cast. Till the dim dawn of day
I heard my castles falling, and the roll
Of angry billows bearing to the sea
The broken timbers of my very soul.
Were all the pent-up waters from the whole
Stupendous solar system to break free,
There are no floods that now can frighten me.

A FABLE

Some cawing Crows, a hooting Owl,
A Hawk, a Canary, an old Marsh-Fowl,
One day all meet together
To hold a caucus and settle the fate
Of a certain bird (without a mate),
A bird of another feather.

"My friends," said the Owl, with a look most wise,
"The Eagle is soaring too near the skies,
In a way that is quite improper;
Yet the world is praising her, so I'm told,
And I think her actions have grown so bold
That some of us ought to stop her."

"I have heard it said," quoth Hawk, with a sigh,
"That young lambs died at the glance of her eye,
And I wholly scorn and despise her.
This, and more, I am told they say,
And I think that the only proper way
Is never to recognize her."

"I am quite convinced," said Crow, with a caw,
"That the Eagle minds no moral law,
She's a most unruly creature."
"She's an ugly thing," piped Canary Bird;
"Some call her handsome—it's so absurd—
She hasn't a decent feature."

Then the old Marsh-Hen went hopping about,
She said she was sure—*she* hadn't a doubt—
Of the truth of each bird's story:
And she thought it a duty to stop her flight,
To pull her down from her lofty height,
And take the gilt from her glory.

But, lo! from a peak on the mountain grand
That looks out over the smiling land
And over the mighty ocean,
The Eagle is spreading her splendid wings—
She rises, rises, and upward swings,
With a slow, majestic motion.

Up in the blue of God's own skies,
With a cry of rapture, away she flies,
Close to the Great Eternal:
She sweeps the world with her piercing sight;
Her soul is filled with the infinite
And the joy of things supernal.

Thus rise forever the chosen of God,
The genius-crowned or the power-shod,
Over the dust-world sailing;
And back, like splinters blown by the winds,
Must fall the missiles of silly minds,
Useless and unavailing.

CPSIA information can be obtained at www.ICGtesting.com
Printed in the USA
243206LV00002B/243/P

9 781604 443448